How can we find out what was happening in Central and Western Europe over 3,000 years ago? At that date there were no written records, but there is still much evidence to be looked at. **Archaeologists** can uncover evidence and can make scientific studies of ancient remains. They have discovered that the period between about 1200 and 700 **BCE** was a time of great change. Instead of burying the ashes of their dead in pottery jars or urns, some groups began to bury their dead in graves, along with bronze weapons, rich jewellery or even **chariots**. This evidence can give us clues to how these people lived. After about 700 BCE, goods made of iron – the amazing new metal that was now being worked in Europe – also began to appear in graves.

This was the dawn of the Celtic Iron Age. Archaeologists call these early years the **Hallstatt** period, named after a site in Austria, which was typically Celtic. A new phase of Celtic culture, based upon the use of iron, dates from about 450 BCE, and is named **La Tène** after an archaeological site in Switzerland. Celtic languages and customs spread far and wide through Europe at this time. Language and customs were sometimes passed on by invasion or **migration** (the movement of peoples), but often they spread as a result of trade or shared inventions.

Towards the end of the La Tène period, the Celts began to be attacked on all sides. Germanic tribes were moving southwards and westwards towards the River Rhine , while the armies of the Roman Empire were marching north from Italy. The Roman army proved to be an unstoppable force.

This Celtic bronze shield was found in the River Thames, in London. It is over 2,000 years old and may have been used for ceremonies rather than in battle.

'...*For the Rive Ister [the Danube] crosses the whole of Europe, rising amongst the Celts ...and the Celts are beyond the Pillars of Hercules [the Straits of Gibraltar]...*'

Herodotus, a Greek historian who lived from about 485 to 425 BCE, makes it clear that Celts were found right across Europe.

1200 BCE	The Celtic way of life in Central Europe begins.
700 BCE	The Hallstatt phase begins.
530 BCE	The date of a magnificent burial of a Celtic chieftain near Hochdorf an der Enz in southwestern Germany.
450 BCE	The La Tène phase of Celtic culture.
390 BCE	A Celtic people called the **Gauls** sack Rome.
58 BCE	Roman general Julius Caesar invades the lands of the Gauls.

Who were the Gaels and the Britons?

Nobody knows when Celtic languages first took root in the British Isles. It is possible that distant ancestors of the Celts introduced early forms of the speech in the Bronze Age, perhaps 3,000 or 4,000 years ago. However, the languages may have arrived much later, during the Iron Age. We do know that the full Celtic culture spread through the British Isles after about 600 BCE. Britain may have become Celtic chiefly as the result of trade and contact. The Celtic lifestyle was simply the way in which most people lived in Western Europe at this time.

Maiden Castle is a massive hill fort covering 19 hectares of land near Dorchester in England. Much of it dates from the Celtic Iron Age, and was raised between about 600 and 300 BCE. It was the headquarters of a British tribe called the Durotriges.

'Most of the island [Britain] is flat and overgrown with forests, although many of its districts are hilly. It produces grain, cattle, gold, silver and iron. These things, accordingly, are exported from the island, as also hides, and slaves and dogs that are by their nature suitable for hunting …
Besides some small islands round about Britain, there is also a large island, Ierne [Ireland] which stretches parallel to Britain …'

Strabo, a Greek geographer and traveller, lived from about 64 BCE and described the British Isles.

Contents

Words in **bold** can be found in the glossary on page 30. The history detective Sherlock Bones, will help you to find clues and collect evidence about the Celts. Wherever you see one of Sherlock's paw-prints, you will find a mystery to solve. The answers can be found on page 31.

Who are the Celts?

Various peoples think of themselves as Celts today. They live on the far western coasts of Europe and include the Scots, Manx, Irish, Welsh, Cornish, Bretons and Galicians. Over 2,000 years ago the Celtic world covered a very large area. It spread out from Central Europe to Turkey in the east and to Spain in the west.

Many different peoples and **tribes** belonged to this ancient **culture**. They never considered themselves to be a single race or nation, but they did share a common culture, or way of life. The ancient Greeks, who were often attacked by them, called them all 'Celts', or *Keltoi*. Historians later picked up the term 'Celts', as a useful way of describing these varied groups. Many of these people spoke languages that were related to each other. These became known as 'Celtic' languages.

The Gauls lived in northern Italy, the Alps and France. The Britons were the people of Britain (who also settled in that part of France still known as Brittany). The Gaels lived in Ireland (and later also settled parts of Scotland and West Wales). Celt-Iberians lived in Spain and Portugal and the Galatians lived in Turkey.

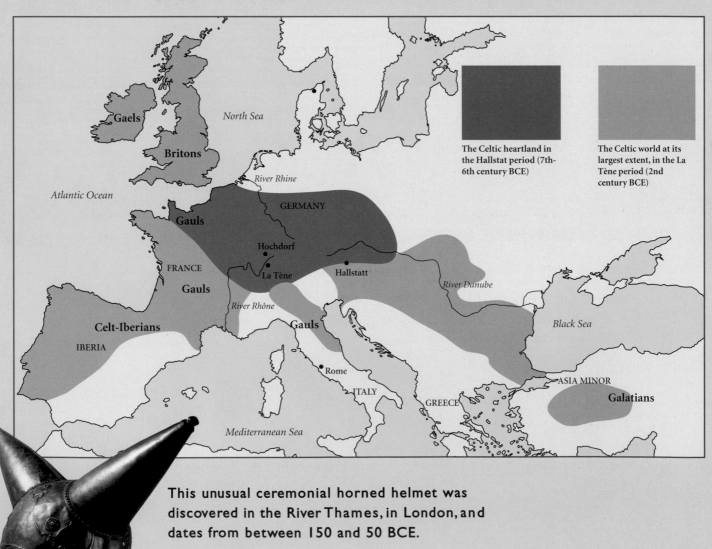

The Celtic heartland in the Hallstat period (7th-6th century BCE)

The Celtic world at its largest extent, in the La Tène period (2nd century BCE)

This unusual ceremonial horned helmet was discovered in the River Thames, in London, and dates from between 150 and 50 BCE.

This life-sized sandstone head, found on a farm in North Wales, may have represented a local god. It was carved in the Celtic Iron Age.

Some warrior bands from northern Gaul or Iberia (Spain) probably did settle in parts of Britain and Ireland between about 600 and 200 BCE and these incomers would also have helped to spread the Celtic culture. Southern and eastern parts of Britain were certainly invaded by Belgic warriors sometime before 100 BCE. These warriors were Celts from the lands between the River Loire and Rhine River, in northeastern Gaul.

Most invasions and migrations were probably local and on a small scale. There was no big shift of population across the English Channel or the Irish Sea. Many of the local population in the Celtic age, most of them red-haired and pale-skinned, others fair or dark, were descended from people who had already been living in the British Isles for thousands of years. They now lived the Celtic life and spoke Celtic languages, so we call them Celts.

The Celts of the British Isles formed two main groups. The Celts living in Ireland were the **Gaels**, and the language they spoke is called *Goidelic*. Those living in Britain were the **Britons**, and the language they spoke is called *Brythonic*. These two languages were related to each other. You can find out quite a lot about Britain and Ireland at this time by reading the work of ancient Greek and Roman writers. They tell us how the islands were divided into many tribal lands. Tribes fought endlessly with each other, raiding each other's territory and stealing cattle. Sometimes tribes banded together in an alliance, especially when faced with an outside threat. However, even when the mighty Romans invaded, there were still some divisions among the Celts.

DETECTIVE WORK

Look at a modern map of Great Britain and Ireland. Can you find place names of Celtic origin? Look out for the following bits of words:

PEN (head) e.g. Penrith
KIL (church) e.g. Kilmarnock
AVON (river) e.g. Avonmouth
CAR or **CAER** (fort) e.g. Caernarfon
LLAN (religious enclosure) e.g. Llanellli
GLAS (green) e.g. Glasgow
POL (pool) e.g. Polzeath
BALLY, BAILE, BEL (town) e.g. Ballycastle
TRE (town) e.g. Treborth
DIN, DEN, DON (stronghold, city) e.g. Maiden Castle

Who were the rulers of the Celtic world?

Each of the Celts' tribal lands had a powerful ruler, who was a leader in battle. Some British kings ruled over larger groups of tribes. Cunobelinus was king of the Catuvellauni tribe, whose capital was at St Albans. Coming to the throne in about 5 CE, he also won control over the Trinovantes, while his son conquered another tribe, the Atrobates. Among the Gaels, the regional kings declared loyalty to a High King of all Ireland.

Women ranked highly in the Celtic world, and it was not unusual for a queen to inherit the throne and lead warriors into battle. Cartimandua, queen of the Brigantes, ruled a large area of what is now Yorkshire, from about 43 CE to 69 CE.

Celtic rulers came only from the highest social class, which was powerful and wealthy. It included the tribe's leading warriors. Sons of lesser nobles were sent to live in the households of more powerful relatives when they were still children, to be trained in warfare. Daughters were sent to be trained in needlework and other skills too. This system of fostering strengthened loyalties within the tribe.

These gold coins were issued by Vercingetorix, a Gaulish leader who fought the Romans and died in captivity in 46 BCE.

Coins were introduced to Britain by the Belgic tribes and were soon being produced for kings in the southeast, such as Cunobelinus.

Other members of this upper class were the **bards**. Bards were official poets and composers, who sang about heroic deeds, praising the bravery of the king. The **Druids** also came from the same top social class. Druids were priests of the ancient Celtic religion, who did not fight. They were scholars who had to learn a

Torcs, open collars made of gold and silver, were worn by Celtic nobles and rulers. This one is displayed in the British Museum, London.

DETECTIVE WORK

In the 1980s, human remains were discovered at Lindow Moss in Cheshire, England. Tests showed one man had lived sometime between 2 BCE and 119 CE. As happens sometimes, his body had been preserved in a bog. Archaeologists thought he had probably been killed as part of a religious ritual. His hair, beard and fingernails were all neatly trimmed, so he had probably belonged to the upper classes. It was clear he had never done rough work with his hands or fought in battles.

See if you can find out anything else about the excavation of Lindow Moss.

great deal of secret **lore** and rituals. They also advised the king or queen, made laws and were sent from one tribe to another to talk about war and peace or alliances. Some Druids were so important that even the king had to wait for them to speak first.

The middle classes included free citizens, who were landowners and farmers. Some made gold jewellery, while others were **blacksmiths**, hammering out iron tools and weapons. The lower classes worked as labourers and had no land, no freedom and few rights. However, the labourers were better off than the slaves, who were captured and brought back in chains from raids on other tribes. Slaves would be sold, or put to work on the land.

The discovery of this ancient body, preserved in a bog at Lindow Moss, Cheshire since the Celtic Iron Age, presented archaeologists with a real puzzle.

Who do you think the Lindow Man might have been?

How did the Celts go to war?

Try to imagine what the capital city of a British tribe might be like in 50 BCE. There would be clusters of dwellings, storehouses, workshops and, set apart, a royal hall standing on the top of a great grassy hill. This hill fort is walled with timber and stone, towering above a series of steep ditches and defensive walls of earth. Through the main gate and down the winding track, light wooden chariots with iron-rimmed wheels come thundering in a cloud of dust, to meet an approaching band of warriors.

A pair of small, sturdy horses at full gallop pull each chariot. The charioteer stands at the front, holding the reins. Behind him stands his lord, a warrior armed with javelins (throwing spears). Once the spears have been thrown, the warrior leaps to the ground and fights the enemy hand to hand. He has a **scabbard** attached to a belt around his waist. From it he draws an iron sword (about 55 centimetres long) and slashes at the enemy. With his left hand he grips the handle of a long, oval shield made of wood, hide and iron.

'Cúchulainn:
*Like a great boar
before his herd,
I'll overwhelm you
before these armies,
I'll push you and punish
you to the last of your skill
and then bring down
havoc on your head.*'

This is an extract from a famous Irish tale called *Táin Bó Cuailnge*, (The Cattle-Raid of Cooley). This tale was written in the Middle Ages and imagines two Celtic warriors, Cúchulainn and Ferdia taunting each other.

Other weapons in the thick of the battle include stabbing spears, daggers and whirling slings that send a deadly hail of stones rattling against the enemy shields. Most warriors fight bare-chested. In earlier days, many Celts fought naked. The chief wears a helmet and a shirt of **mail**. These linked iron rings of the shirts may have been the invention of Celtic smiths. Above the cries of battle rises the braying sound of a **carnyx** or war trumpet, sounding victory.

Many Celtic iron swords and spearheads have survived.

As fighters, the Celts had a reputation. They liked to boast and insult the enemy. They were described as quarrelsome, cunning, absolutely fearless and full of bravado. Every warrior wanted to be the hero and claim all the glory. The Celts loved single combat, where each army chose a champion to do battle on their behalf. When the Romans came to Britain, the Celts could not understand these soldiers who had been drilled to fight all together like a killing machine.

🐾 **Which spooky festival celebrated today might have come from the Celts?**

This silver cauldron found at Gundestrup in Denmark is 2,000 years old. One side shows pictures of warriors. Some are blowing the carnyx.

DETECTIVE WORK

The early Celts used to cut off the heads of their enemies and hang them in the temples of their gods. The severed heads were believed to have magical qualities and to be able to speak. Some people believe that a modern festival in which spooky 'heads' are placed in the home had its origins from the Celtic practice. See what you can learn about Celtic festivals from books and the Internet.

What was it like to live in a roundhouse?

Celtic tribes were divided into clans, large groups of people who shared common descent. Within the clans were family groups, whose honour a warrior would defend with his life. Each family would occupy a household made up of huts and outbuildings. In Central and Eastern Europe, the dwellings were rectangular. In Western Europe, including Britain and Ireland, huts were round.

Imagine visiting a roundhouse, picking your way between the muddy pens of cattle and sheep and ignoring the barking of the hounds. The outer walls might be made of timber or stone, depending on what building materials were available locally. They might be 'wattle and daub' (a framework of wooden strips plastered with clay). The high roof is cone-shaped and heavily thatched with straw or reeds. Going inside, you would need to get used to the gloom and your eyes would water in the smoky atmosphere. In the centre of the hut is a hearth, with pots simmering over the embers of a fire. The floor is about 15 metres from side to side and might be made of beaten earth or stone slabs. Sweet-smelling hay or rushes are strewn on the floor. Around the wall are compartments where members of the family may sleep, repair weapons, sew or play dice or board games. Other cubicles are used for storage.

DETECTIVE WORK

Sometimes Celtic settlements were not built beside lakes but actually in them, on small islands, that are known as crannogs. These islands could be artificial and built up from a shallow lake floor. They could be reached by a **causeway**. Why do you think people would choose to build their homes in such a difficult spot?

How do you think the Celts on the crannogs managed for food?

This lake dwelling has been reconstructed at Loch Tay, in Scotland.

'Forest thickets are their 'cities'. They fence round a wide clearing with felled trees and here they make themselves huts and keep their cattle.'

This is Strabo writing once again about the Celts. Large areas of land were fenced off and fortified. During an attack, herds of cattle from outlying farms could be brought in for protection.

A settlement may have looked like this, with a metalworking site in the foreground and a roundhouse with a high thatched roof.

Celtic settlements were closely guarded and the outer gates were shut at night. Some settlements grew up beside the stronghold of a great lord or ruler, where travelling merchants would display their goods, and outside entertainment might include horseracing or wrestling. Smaller settlements were often sited in farmland, isolated in forest clearings or built beside lakes and rivers.

Coracles (small boats made of hide stretched over wickerwork) were used for fishing. Celtic settlements were joined by ancient trackways and paths, along which ponies, chariots or oxcarts could travel. Not until the Romans came were roads properly paved and drained. The Celts were not big city builders like the Romans. The Belgic tribes of southern and eastern Britain did build large fortified towns, which the Romans called oppida. The largest was Camolodunum, which is now called Colchester.

Wattle or wickerwork was made of plaited staves covered in mud.

What did the Celts eat and drink?

Food was cooked in cauldrons suspended over a hearth, or roasted on turning spits. It was eaten with fingers, or with a knife or spoon, from a low table. The Celts were famous for their hospitality. A royal feast was a long and lavish affair, often interrupted by quarrels and tales of the day's hunting. The very best cuts of meat were saved for the bravest warrior, who was awarded the 'hero's portion' – unless someone else claimed it and fought him for it. The Celts drank large quantities of ale and mead, a strong alcoholic drink made from honey. Wine was imported to Britain from Gaul.

The Celts were great hunters, using spears or nets and packs of hounds. Salmon were caught in rivers, wild boars and stags in the forests, and wildfowl in the marshes. Hunting provided food but it was also a favourite pastime and one that could even turn into a magical experience. Celtic tales often told of hunts when the animals changed shape or even became human.

DETECTIVE WORK

Which foods did the Celts not have? Many foods didn't reach Europe until a later age when explorers brought them home. The Irish were later famous for potatoes but at this point these were only grown in unknown lands of South America. Sugar cane was unknown in Iron Age Europe.

🐾 **The Celts did sweeten their food. What do you think they used?**

Hazelnuts were collected for food. The hazel tree was holy to the Druids, and salmon were believed to have magical powers if they ate hazelnuts, which had fallen into a stream.

The Celts loved to eat pork, either from hunted wild boar or from their own herds of pigs, which were famous for their size and aggressiveness.

Celtic farmers raised strong breeds of cattle, which were prized and sometimes fought over. Cattle were a form of currency or money, used to pay for other goods. Oxen were used for ploughing and hauling goods. Goats were raised, too, and tough little sheep, rather like today's Soay breed were also kept. Pigs were allowed to wander in the woods, where they ate acorns. Geese, ducks, chickens and pigeons were also kept. Every farming settlement had its beehives. Farm produce included meat, milk, butter, curds, cheese, honey, beeswax, hides and wool. Foods were preserved in salt or smoked over a fire.

Crops included beans and varieties of wheat (known to archaeologists as emmer and spelt), barley, oats and rye. Grain could be ground into flour with a stone hand-mill called a **quern**, and was used to make loaves of bread, griddle cakes or bannocks and porridge. Apples, hazelnuts and berries formed an important part of the diet, and seaweed and herbs were used in cooking.

Why did the Celts love metal?

Metalworkers were held in great respect by the Celts. Bronze, an alloy or mixture of tin and copper, had been made in the British Isles since about 1700 BCE. The Celts became experts at casting solid bronze in a clay mould and at hammering beautiful patterns into thin sheets of the metal. Iron technology reached the British Isles in about 600 BCE and iron ore (rock which contained iron) could, like tin and copper, be mined locally. Iron was much harder and tougher than bronze, and could be put to many more uses. Blacksmiths sent up clouds of sparks at the village forge. Even everyday objects were beautifully designed works of art with a style that can be identified at once as Celtic.

Firedogs were decorative iron supports used to hold a log on the hearth.

This magnificent cauldron, found in a bog at Gundestrup, was made sometime after 120 BCE. It is the largest piece of silver work of its period. Experts disagree as to where it was made and by whom.

This pot was decorated when the clay was still soft. It was then fired in the ashes of a simple bonfire, which served as a kiln.

Archaeologists have discovered Celtic jewellery and beautiful mirrors of polished bronze. They have found weapons, shield parts, helmets, armour, and parts of chariots including wheel rims and harnesses for the horses. They have excavated practical tools such as axes, billhooks, chisels, saws, hammers, tongs and sickles. They have found hoops to put around wooden barrels, **cauldrons** and cups. They have discovered chains that went around the necks of captive prisoners. They have also found coins and iron bars which may also have been used as currency.

Iron was seen as so marvellous that people across Europe believed this new metal must have magical power. That may be the origin of the more recent custom of nailing a 'lucky' iron horseshoe to the door – to keep away evil spirits or wicked fairies.

The Celts also worked in gold and silver. Arts and crafts in the early period were often crudely finished but were still very powerful, for example, heads of the gods, which were carved in stone or wood. In the later phase of Celtic arts and crafts, there appear very fine, swirling patterns and knot designs. Some of the most wonderful Celtic art shows animals – boars, birds, horses, deer and leaping fish. Many of these creatures were symbols with religious meanings. The Belgic tribes of southern and eastern Britain made pottery on a pottery wheel, as well as glass and enamel, a coloured, glassy coating for metal.

Charcoal and iron ore were placed in small furnaces for smelting.

🐾 Special air pumps were used to keep the furnace fire going. Do you know what they are called?

Who were the Iron Age gods?

Religious belief was at the heart of everyday life in the world of the ancient Celts. The natural world was full of magic and its power filled birds, fish and animals. This spirit bubbled up through springs, wells and lakes. The name 'Druid' is probably linked to the word for 'oak', and knowledge of trees and plants was part of the secret lore of the Druids. Groves of oak trees were holy places. When Britain's Roman invaders reached the Druids' stronghold of Mona (Anglesey) in 61 CE, their troops set fire to the sacred groves and destroyed them.

The Celts raised special religious enclosures, within square-shaped banks of earth. Statues of gods and goddesses were carved from oak or stone. Many represent heads, some with two or three faces. Some gods were local or tribal, but others were found across the Celtic world, such as Cernunnos (the horned god) who was lord of the hunt. He is generally shown with stag's antlers, wearing a torc around his neck. The Irish Morrigan, a crow-goddess who haunted battlefields, was a figure of terror. Offerings were made to the gods and left by springs or thrown into lakes.

The figure on the Gundestrup cauldron is believed to show the Celtic god Cernunnos. He is surrounded by wild animals. In one hand he holds a torc, in the other a snake.

Celtic religious rituals were linked to the great oak trees.

Animals or even humans might be sacrificed at festivals. There were four great festivals in the Celtic year. Imbolc, on 1 February, was sacred to Brigit (who as Brigantia was worshipped as a godddess of northern Britain). Beltain, on 1 May, was a fire festival during which cattle were driven through bonfires. The sacrifce was made to help the crops grow and the herds breed. Lughnasa, lasting for a month from 1 August to 1 September, was a harvest festival, in honour of the god, Lugh. Samhain, on 1 November, was a scary festival, when spirits of the dead were believed to walk the night.

Celts believed in a life after death that was just as real as life in this world. It took place in an underworld, the land of the fairies, or according to others on an island far away to the west. Irish tales tell of *Tír na nÓg*, the land of eternal youth, and British tales talk of Avalon, the golden 'land of apples'.

'The Druids…consider nothing more sacred than the mistletoe and the tree that it grows on, so long as it is an oak…Mistletoe is actually very rare on an oak tree, and when it is found it is gathered with great ceremony. In the first place the collection must take place on the sixth day of the moon…A priest dressed in white climbs the tree, cuts the mistletoe with a golden hook and catches it on a white cloak…'

A Roman scholar called Pliny the Elder wrote about the Druids in 77 CE.

DETECTIVE WORK

Llyn Cerrig Bach is a small lake on the Isle of Anglesey in North Wales. In 1943, the runway of an airfield was being extended into the boggy land around this lake. An old iron chain was attached to a tractor for haulage during the work. Someone noticed that this was actually an ancient Celtic chain that would have been used for prisoners or slaves. Archaeologists excavated the bog and made an amazing find. They found a Celtic treasure hoard that included spears, harnesses, shield bosses, chariots, wheels and an Irish trumpet. It was clear that these items were thrown in the lake almost 2,000 years ago. You could try to learn about other Celtic excavation sites and see what kinds of objects were found.

🐾 **Why do you think the Celts threw their possessions into Llyn Cerrig Bach?**

What happened to Britain when the Romans came?

Between 58 BCE and 52 BCE the Roman general, Julius Caesar, conquered the Gauls, the Celtic tribes living in what is now France. During this military campaign, in the summer of 55 BCE, Caesar crossed the English Channel and landed in Britain with about 12,000 troops. He met with fierce resistance. The following year he returned with 32,000 soldiers and this time defeated the Catuvellauni tribe. Before leaving, he forced other tribes of southeastern Britain to pay tribute to Rome. That was not the end of the story, however. In 43 CE, the Romans returned with an army of 40,000 men. And this time they intended to stay.

DETECTIVE WORK

Underneath the city of London, archaeologists have discovered a thick layer of burnt material in the soil. It covers up Roman coins and pottery dating from before 60 CE.
What event might have caused such a great fire? Who do you think was responsible?

Celtic Tribes of Britain and Ireland

'On the shore stood the opposing army with its dense array of armed warriors, while between the ranks dashed women dressed in black like the Furies, with hair dishevelled, waving torches. All round the Druids, lifting up their hands to the heavens and pouring forth dreadful curses, scared our soldiers…'

The Roman historian, Tacitus, described the Roman attack on the island of Mona (Anglesey) in 61 CE.

Within about four years, the Roman troops were in control of southern Britain, but it took them another 30 or more to conquer the west. In 60-61 CE, there was a savage rebellion in the east, led by Boudicca, queen of the Iceni tribe. Her warriors destroyed Colchester, London and St Albans before she was halted in a savage battle. She killed herself by taking poison rather than admit defeat. In 84 CE, the Caledonian tribes of what is now Scotland were defeated by the Romans. 'They make a wilderness and call it peace' were the bitter words of Calgacus, war leader of the Caledonians. The Romans built a defensive wall from the River Tyne to the Solway Firth, but they never held down the lands beyond it for very long, and they never attacked the Gaels in Ireland.

Boudicca was the wife of Prasutagus, king of the Iceni tribe.

The Romans built roads and towns, law courts and grand country houses called villas. Many Britons now worked as farm labourers on Roman estates. Others continued to live in their villages, sometimes selling crops, hides or metalwork to the Romans. Some Roman soldiers took British wives when they retired. Many of the British upper classes took up the Roman way of life, learning Latin and wearing Roman clothes. Roman and Celtic styles of art, even their gods and goddesses, became mixed up. This combined culture is called Romano-British.

Roman power weakened in the 200s and 300s. Gaels from Ireland attacked western coasts, and Germanic tribes called Saxons attacked in the east and south. There were troubles in Gaul too, and in 410 CE the Romans withdrew from Britain. By 476 CE, Rome itself, the western capital of the mighty Roman Empire, had fallen to Germanic invaders.

55-54 BCE	Julius Caesar's invasion of southern Britain.
43 CE	The Roman conquest of Britain begins.
60-61 CE	Boudicca's rebellion against the Romans.
122 CE	Building of Hadrian's wall begins across northern Britain.
410 CE	Roman troops start to pull out of Britain.
476	Rome falls.

For many years Hadrian's wall marked the northwestern limit of the mighty Roman empire. Its ruins may still be seen today.

What happened when the Romans left?

After the Romans withdrew their troops, the Britons set up many small kingdoms of their own. These soon came under attack from the Picts of the far north, and from a Gaelic group known as Scoti, who founded a kingdom called Dal Ríada in western Scotland. Germanic invaders, called Angles and Saxons, poured across the North Sea. They founded kingdoms too and gradually won control of what would soon be called England.

The Britons fought the Saxons every step of the way. In the early 500s, a legendary hero called Arthur may have led them. Tales later described him as a great king, but if he did exist he would have been more like a brave war leader hired by the kings or a high king. As the Saxons advanced, many Britons fled westwards, some escaping from Cornwall to Brittany. In the far west, British kingdoms did manage to survive. These western Britons began to call themselves *Cymry,* meaning 'fellow-countrymen'. The Saxons called them 'Welsh', meaning 'strangers'.

Missionaries, such as St Patrick, now spread the Christian faith, which had taken root during Roman times, rapidly through Britain and Ireland. Monks lived simple lives in small stone cells and the sacred wells of the ancient Celts were now used for baptism. A Gael called St Columba, in 563 CE,

This beautiful decoration of the capital letter P is from the Book of Kells, scriptures hand-written by Christian monks in about 800 CE.

The ogham script below was used like an alphabet by the Gaels.

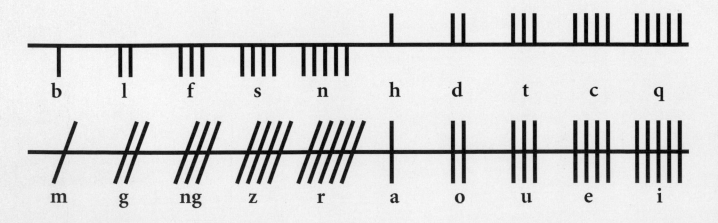

b l f s n h d t c q

m g ng z r a o u e i

This silver chalice, a cup used in Christian worship was found at Ardagh in Ireland. It is decorated with gold, brass and enamel and dates from the 800s CE.

DETECTIVE WORK

Ogham was a sort of alphabet carved on Irish stones from around 300 CE to 600 CE. Irish settlers also carved ogham in Scotland and West Wales. It was made up of lines like those on page 24. You can use it to make up modern words in the ancient alphabet. See if you can write your name with the alphabet of the Celts (see page 24).

founded a famous monastery on the Scottish island of Iona. After 597 CE, the Angles and Saxons also began to convert to the Christian faith.

By the 700s and 800s, a wonderful new period of Celtic culture was thriving in Ireland and Dal Ríada. Jewellers made fantastic brooches, chalices (cups used in Christian worship) and croziers (ceremonial staffs used by bishops). Monks wrote out the Christian scriptures in beautiful handwriting and decorated the letters and margins of their books with intricate pictures and patterns. Stone crosses were carved. At the same time the Britons (or Welsh) were producing poetry of great beauty and power. This great flowering of the arts had its roots in the world of the ancient Celts.

New armies of invaders were soon pouring into the British Isles. Then followed centuries of hardship and loss of freedom for the Celtic peoples. However, along the western coasts of Europe, the descendants of those ancient Celts somehow adapted to the changing world – and survived.

433 CE	St Patrick in Ireland.
500 CE	Gaelic kingdom of Dal Ríada.
c537 CE	Supposed death of King Arthur at Battle of Camlan.
563 CE	St Columba founds monastery at Iona.
600 CE	Earliest known poetry in Welsh.
650 CE	Start of a golden age of art in Ireland.

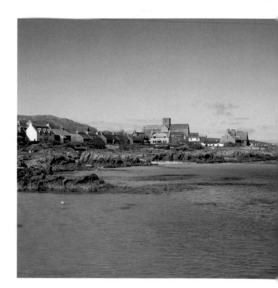

The Scottish island of Iona is a visited by Christian pilgrims today and is a spiritual centre.

How do we know about the Celts?

Celtic treasures fill museums in **Great Britain** and **Ireland**. They have survived because they are mostly made from metal, pottery or stone. They have been carefully excavated, measured, listed and restored by archaeologists. Human remains also give up many secrets. Bones found at **Maiden Castle** show just how warriors were killed when fighting the Romans. Some human bodies recovered from bogs have been preserved in the damp peat. Radiocarbon dating tells archaeologists just when these people lived. Examination may also show what food they ate and how they dressed.

Both Britons and Gaels left lasting marks on the landscape, in the form of field patterns, fortifications and housing. Some hill forts are older than the Celtic period, but ditches and mounds seen on a hill or headland often shows that they were occupied during the Iron Age. Spectacular examples include Maiden Castle in Dorset,

Chysauster in Cornwall was a farming settlement which was occupied until the third century CE. It was made of eight houses, as well as outbuildings.

England, and Tre'r Ceiri in North Wales. In Scotland, the Picts built tall stone towers called **brochs** and many still stand, as on Mousa, one of the Shetland Islands. Where stone was used in building houses, their circular walls and foundations may also still be seen. Chysauster in Cornwall is one example, built by people of the Dumnonii tribe from about 100 BCE onwards.

The ancient Greeks and Romans often wrote about the Celts. We cannot always be sure that they were telling the truth about people who were their enemies, but they do describe Celtic customs, gods, ways of fighting and everyday life in great detail. Many of these texts can still be read today. From the 600s onwards, we also have the texts written down by Christian monks. Some of the most useful information about the ancient Celts is found in poetry and tales written down much later in the Middle Ages. Examples include the Irish *Táin Bó Cuailnge*, which tells of the hero Cúchulainn, or the magical tales of the Welsh *Mabinogi*. Parts of these are very old and must have been passed down by word of mouth from the early days of the Celts.

This piece of bronze dates from the first or second century BCE. It was part of a horse's harness and was decorated with enamel. It was used in Gaul but may have been made in Britain.

An archaeologist strips off the surface of the ground while excavating the site of an Iron Age farming settlement.

Your project

Aproject on the Celts is exciting, because it could take in as much as 3,000 years of history. It might include some research into Celtic languages and names, some arts and crafts in the ancient Celtic tradition or even some cooking.

Sherlock Bones says you can be a language detective! You can discover a lot about Celtic history by looking at words in Celtic languages and seeing how they connect with each other or with languages such as English. Many Celtic words can be found by looking on the Internet. The Brythonic language of the ancient Britons developed into Welsh, Cornish and Breton in the early Middle Ages. The Goidelic language of the Gaels developed into Manx, Irish and Scots Gaelic at the same time.

Some words are similar in all of these languages. Take the word 'cow', for example, the Welsh word is *buwch*, the Cornish is *bugh* and the Breton is *bu'och*. The Manx word is *booa* and the word in both Irish and Scots Gaelic is *bó*. These are all Celtic languages and are part of a large language family that stretches from Ireland to India. It is called Indo-European. It should come as little surprise that the Latin word *bos* means ox, from which comes the English 'bovine' which means 'like an ox' or 'to do with cattle.'

Project Ideas

- In the 1800s and 1900s, Celtic people from Britain and Ireland made new homes for themselves around the world, from New Zealand to South America. They named many towns after places from home. Using an atlas or the Internet can you find place names in the UK or Republic of Ireland that are used again in other countries? Start with looking for Aberdeen, Bangor and Truro and then see if you can see others. You could mark these on a map or put them in a chart.

- Celtic designs are still used on jewellery and other things today. Look at the Celtic jewellery in the picture (left) and see if you can draw some of the designs on a piece of white card and design your own Celtic jewellery.

- You can even make a recipe from the ancient Celtic world and bake some Scottish oatcakes that are still popular today. You could also try to find some other traditional recipes from Ireland, Scotland, Cornwall or Wales that have their roots in the ancient Celtic world. To make these oatcakes you will need some help from an adult to use the hob, oven and to boil the water.

You will need:

60 g medium oatmeal
60 g wholemeal flour
1 tablespoon of lard (this is what the Celts would have used but you can use cooking margarine if you like)
¼ teaspoon bicarbonate of soda
pinch of salt
3 tablespoons boiling water
(serves 2)

1. Preheat the oven to 200°C
2. Put the oatmeal, flour, salt and bicarbonate of soda in a mixing bowl, together with the lard or margarine (melted) and the hot water. Mix this into a firm dough.
3. Sprinkle a little flour on to a board and roll out the dough until about ½ cm thick.
4. Cut out the dough circles with the rim of a water glass or a biscuit cutter.
5. Line a tray with baking paper. Put the dough circles on the baking paper and bake for 15 minutes in the oven.

Let the oatcakes cool before you eat them. You can eat the oatcakes with butter, cheese and apples.

Glossary

alloy A mixure of two metals. Bronze is an alloy of tin and copper.

archaeologist Someone who studies ancient remains.

bard An offical poet in ancient Celtic society.

BCE The years Before the Common Era, or for Christians: the years before Christ's birth.

blacksmith Someone who makes or repairs iron objects.

Briton One of the ancient people of Great Britain, who later also settled in Brittany.

broch A strong, stone tower built by the Picts, the peoples of far northern Britain who were never conquered by Rome.

Bronze Age A period in any part of the world when making bronze was the most important technology,

carnyx A long, upright trumpet used in battle by the ancient Celts.

cauldron A large metal cooking pot.

causeway A raised path built on a shallow lake floor or across a shore.

CE Common Era, or for Christians: the years after Christ's birth.

Celt-Iberian One of the Celtic or part-Celtic peoples of ancient Spain and Portugal.

chariot A light horse-drawn cart, used for warfare, hunting or racing.

coracle A small, round boat made of hide stretched over wickerwork. It is steered and driven by a paddle.

culture The way of life, customs and traditions of a group of people.

Druid A priest, scholar, law-maker and envoy amongst the ancient Celts.

forge A workshop where metal was heated and hammered into objects.

Gael One of the ancient people of Ireland, who later also settled in parts of Scotland.

Gaul 1) One of the ancient people who occupied France, the Alps and northern Italy in the Celtic Iron Age. 2) The land of the Gauls.

grove A group of trees or a small wood.

Hallstatt An archaeological site in Austria which gave its name to the earliest period of Celtic culture.

hill fort A large hilltop settlement defended from attack by ditches and barriers, popular in the Celtic Iron Age.

Iron Age A period in any part of the world when iron working was the most important technology.

La Tène An archaeological site in Switzerland which gave its name to the period of Celtic culture just before the Roman conquests.

loom A framework on which cloth is woven.

lore A special wisdom or knowledge usually concerned with traditional beliefs.

mail Armour made from small, interlinking iron rings.

mead A strong, sweet alcoholic drink made from honey.

migration A large scale movement of people from one land or region to another.

peat A spongy layer of plant remains found waterlogged in a bog.

quern A hand-mill made from two discs of rough stone, used for grinding grain into flour.

radiocarbon dating A way of dating ancient materials such as wood or fibre by measuring how radioactive they are.

sacred holy.

scabbard The sheath which holds and protects the blade of a sword.

spit An iron prong used for roasting meat over a fire.

staves Wooden bars or rods.

torc A collar, generally of gold or bronze, open at the front and worn around the neck.

tribe A group of people sharing the same culture. They are loyal to a chief or ruler.

yarn Spun thread, used for weaving cloth.

Answers

Page 9:   He was probably a Druid.
Page 11:   The festival is Halloween.
Page 14:   The Celts would eat fish from the lake.
Page 16:   The ancient Celts used natural honey to sweeten their food.
Page 19:   The special air pumps used to keep fires going are called bellows.
Page 21:   People would have thrown their most treasured possessions in the lake as special offerings to the gods.

Further Information

Books to read

The Ancient Celts by Patricia Calvert (Franklin Watts, 2005)
Find Out About the Celts by Fiona Macdonald (Southwater, 2002)
Britain Through the Ages: Celts by Hazel Mary Martell (Evans Brothers 2003)
The Facts About the Celts by Robert Hull (Wayland, 2007)
British Heritage: The Celts in Britain by Dereen Taylor (Wayland, 2007)

Websites

http://europeanhistory.about.com/od/celts/Celts.htm
http://www.bbc.net.uk/history/ancient/british_prehistory/
http://www.britainexpress.com/History/Celtic_Britain.htm
Note to parents and teachers: Every effort has been made by the publishers to ensure that these websites are suitable for children. However, because of the nature of the Internet, it is impossible to guarantee that the contents of these sites will not be altered. We strongly advise that Internet access is supervised by a responsible adult.

Places to visit

The British Museum, Great Russell Street, London, WC1B 3DG
The National Museum of Wales, Cathays Park, Cardiff, CF10 3NP
St Fagans: National History Museum, St Fagans, Cardiff, CF5 6XB
National Museum of Scotland, Chambers Street, Edinburgh, EH1 1JF
The National Museum of Ireland, Archaeology & History, Kildare Street, Dublin 2

Sites to visit

Din Lligwy, Anglesey, Wales
Chysauster, Cornwall, England
Scottish Crannog Centre, Perthshire, Scotland
Maiden Castle Hill fort, Dorset, England
Hill of Tara, Ireland

Index